Dedication

To our boys, Jack and Thomas.

on the farm DEER RECOVERY

Published by Lee Lamb, Northern Southland, New Zealand

ISBN 978-0-473-33981-4

First impression 2015 printed by Alliance Printers Ltd

Special thanks to

Peter Spencer-Bower and
Alpine Helicopters for providing photos.

It's an exciting day at Winding Creek Station –
the dogs are heading off to a deer sale!
They are going with the farmer to buy a new stag
he has picked from a brochure in the mail.

BNZ
DEER
SALE

The farmer arrived and took a seat, then he waited for the sale to begin.

There were lots of stags to choose from - but only one that was for him!

Finally the stag came out. He was big and strong and bold.

The farmer bid as far as he could, then the auctioneer yelled – "SOLD!"

EXIT
DEER SALE
RED DEER FARM ANNUAL AUCTION
BUYER # 90

The first thing that had to happen
before the stag could leave the shed –
he had to be squeezed tightly in the crush
so the velvet could be removed from his head.
This didn’t hurt him as the vet gave him medicine
before the velvet was cut off with the saw.
With the heavy weight lifted from him,
he could now easily fit through the door!

VE

The stag was delivered to the farm on a big truck that carries deer.

Everyone gathered around for a glimpse as he appeared.

The stag happily trotted down the lane,
to join up with the mob of hinds.
Everything was new for him there,
but he didn't seem to mind.

Later on black clouds began to build up, and a big storm rolled in that night.

The farmer worried about his stock, but couldn't check them till first light.

The last place a nervous cat wants to be in a storm
is outside in the rain, walking alone across the lawn.

Especially when you have a dog like Jack,
who lets out a sneaky bark - almost giving him a heart attack!

When morning came they set off to check the animals, tracks and fences too.
The dogs sat amongst the fencing gear and waited to see what they could do.

As they came around the corner they could see a landslide and a fallen tree.
Both had come down and flattened the fence where the deer used to be.

WCS10

The deer had escaped in fright
during the storm the night before.
The farmer and the dogs searched for them
but they weren't on the farm anymore.

The farmer quickly rang his friend
who was flying his helicopter next door.
He said "we need to do some deer recovery,
have you done this before?"

Within minutes the helicopter arrived and they set off to find the deer.

The farmer suggested where to look, but they could be anywhere!

Luckily the mob was all together on a hill block not too far away.

The hinds came back quite easily, but the new stag decided to stay.

They tried for hours to get him back in but the stag would not agree
that home was in that ➜ direction and that was where he should be!

They decided in the end that netting him was the best option.
This also meant jumping out of the helicopter and landing right on top of him!

They had success on their first attempt,
and the stag was returned to the farm.
The farmer was glad that the stag was home,
and pleased they had come to no harm.

PSB
PSB

With the deer safely in a new paddock, it was time for the cleanup to begin.
Everyone came out to lend a hand and they were eager to get stuck in.

The digger cleared the landslide away and it was used to fill wallows made by the deer.
The wood from the tree was put to use too, making plenty of firewood for next year.

CAT
CAT

The farmer was grateful for all the help, and that the stag was safely recovered.

The stag never went over another fence – it's far nicer in a paddock, he discovered!

About us

Lee, Jamie, Jack and Thomas live on a deer, cattle and sheep farm in Wanaka, New Zealand.

Glossary

Stag – a male deer

Hind – female deer

Wallow – deer really enjoying playing in water and mud! This can mean that they sometimes make big muddy holes in paddocks called wallows.

Net Gun – is a device that fires a net from a helicopter over a fleeing deer to capture it. It can be hand held or mounted on the skid of the helicopter. It is a NZ invention.

Crush – a crush is a hydraulic device which is manually operated to squeeze deer and restrain them safely.

Velvet – Velvet is growing antler and it is grown annually by the male deer. The antlers grow rapidly out from the pedicles on the deer's head. The velvet contains a lot of blood and nerve supply. The soft antlers are very sensitive at this time and are covered in a soft velvety hair.

Removing deer velvet – Velvet is harvested to be used for medicinal purposes. It also must be removed for transport so that the sensitive velvet antler isn't damaged during transport which would cause the deer pain. The velvetting procedure may only be carried out by a trained professional or by a vet. They give special drugs to the deer to ensure the procedure is pain free.

Deer recovery – Deer farming is relatively new and was only legalised in NZ in 1969. In the early days of deer farming some very brave people used to shoot nets out and then jump from helicopters to catch wild deer. The deer were captured alive and released on to deer farms to breed from. This was a very dangerous but exciting job!